SANA

POEMS

Maria Bolaños

Sampaguita Press

Sana
Published by Sampaguita Press
1298 Fleming Ave
San Jose, CA 95127

www.SampaguitaPress.com

For information about permission to reproduce selections from this book, please contact SampaguitaPress@gmail.com.

Cover and book design by: Maria Bolaños
Cover art: *Sayang at Sana* by Francesca Alarcon

ISBN 979-8-9857712-0-6 (paperback)
ISBN 979-8-9857712-1-3 (ebook)

This publication is made possible by funding provided in part by the Yerba Buena Center for the Arts and other generous contributions from our readers. We offer our heartfelt thanks for your support.

"Maria Bolaños' poems give soundscape and shelter to flowers expanding, to clouds migrating, to pressing pacing onto earth, and to Filipina women whose experiences are lived and more than tsismis. *Sana* is a pedagogy of locating origin stories that name the roots and flowers of familial, historical, and epistemological pain. In this expansive and imaginative chapbook, there are matriarchs and monsters asserting with scores of light and length, 'I am no less than you.'"
—**JANICE LOBO SAPIGAO**, *like a solid to a shadow*

"I've been whispering, 'wow,' exclaiming, tearing up, smiling to myself all through this book: *Sana*. I've turned my eyes inward to nod or shake my head in recognition, pushed back from the table and shouted, 'yes!' At energy and syntax fresh and ancient. At how Maria Bolaños has crafted poems who turn future from an unreachable past—'that nothing is how I remember'—and greet into a present where 'the hills conspire with us.' These are poems who know what shapes they needed to be. Salamat. This is language in the work of making a needed language. In it I feel the tectonics and genders and violences of longing, the ways this poet teaches us how they can be shifted. And I couldn't be more grateful. *Sana* is a book to read and read again. Bolaños is a poet to seek out and invite."
—**HARI ALLURI**, *The Flayed City*

"These quiet, anticolonial first histories demonstrate the expansive intimacies of Filipina mythos—ghosts of a black market imaginary, and the small threats of tomorrow."
—**JASON MAGABO PEREZ**, *This is for the mostless*

"If the woman is a warrior, then *Sana* is the battlefield on which she triumphs. Each poem tells the story of the fearless island woman conquering amidst the waves of erasure. When one would shy away, *Sana* urges us to look at atrocities that have torn the woman apart—watch as she stitches herself together again. Weaving fantasy, tradition, and culture to make a patchwork quilt that sings a song all should tune their ears to. In *Sana*, a woman is everything from a candle, a cactus, an island, the raging fire, a waging war, and even the maker of the world. And what a world she makes. Each poem in *Sana* creates a mythos and breathes life into the fight to keep our heads above water. *Sana* begs for you to bask in pools of unlearning and reclamation of culture, tongue, and body. This collection takes the reader on a journey of salt and ocean, of coconut, mango, and fish, where the woman climbs her way out of the impossible mountain oppression has tried to bury her beneath."
—**KHALISA RAE**, *Ghost in a Black Girl's Throat*

"*Sana* draws us into the depths of wounds inflicted by colonial imperialism, both back in the motherland and as members of the diaspora in a new home. These poems find tender forgiveness for both family and countries in a way that strips the reader's expectations raw. A must read."
—**CHRIS L. BUTLER**, *BLERD* and *Sacrilegious*

"Bolaños captures the essence of the shared memory that unites Filipinx people across the globe with beautiful and haunting language. *Sana* will take readers on a journey through landscapes both real and imagined."
—**ZACHARY FR ANDERSON**, *AsAm News*

"These poems reach out to those with a complicated relationship with their cultural identity. In quiet strokes, Bolaños invites us to revisit our difficult personal histories through lived experience and loss, history and mythology. In the face of loss and oppression, each poem is resilient, resistant and are grounding words for many Filipino/a/x living through similar experiences across the diaspora."
—**NATHALIE DE LOS SANTOS**, *Ricepaper Magazine* and PilipinxPages

"*Sana* is a poetry collection that validates on the page the experiences of colonialism, immigration and what it means to be a part of the diaspora. Bolaños' lyrical prose takes you for a ride from a busy Manila street, her childhood home to Southern California."
—**TIFFANY TARAMPI**, PilipinxPages

"*Sana* reads like a modernized epic insofar that every poem pushes forth a narrative that is a grounded, dreamlike, and transformative journey. Maria Bolaños' poems are in part reclamation and in part harrowing images and statements of reinvention, memories, and relationships at large. It demands careful attention, especially in the dizzying arrangement of 'In the Last Days of the Kingdom': 'A skyline cuts uneven teeth / an animal's mouth in one long and pleading gasp.'"
—**RACHAEL CROSBIE**, *Trick Mirror or Your Computer Screen*

"Throughout *Sana*, Bolaños invites you down a path of both intimate quiets and worlds ignited by historical flint, practicing remembering as a magma-like meditation. The power of naming in this collection not only comes from careful observation of self but from melting into and alongside the surrounding people and places, showing us how nature is just as lively as our loved ones. This collection is radically soft, a spirited family reunion pieced together on the page, come to life."
—**CZAERRA GALICINAO UCOL**, Luya Poetry

"*Sana* is an absolutely exemplary piece of art from a Pinay's heart. Carefully crafted words detail the impact of intergenerational trauma, care for the motherland, homage to family, and much more. With author Maria Bolaños's strengthened writing voice, readers will find themselves getting lost in *Sana*'s waves of emotion: the one above all being love."
—**ISABEL ANGELES**, The Walang Hiya Project

A Note to the Reader

The works contained in this chapbook are of subjects real and fantastical, but all equally true.

These poems seek to discuss the burdens of a family living in a house of intergenerational trauma; there will be mentions of corporal punishment, toxic family dynamics, death, and the Covid-19 pandemic.

These poems will also explore the continued harm of 500 years of colonialism in the motherland known as the Philippines, and the oppression and loss felt by her children in the diaspora. There will be mentions of racism, police systems and cultural gatekeeping, anti-Asian violence and hate, and physical assault on brown women's bodies.

Kaibigan, please remember to be gentle with yourself, and read with care.

For my family,

the ones who hold me

in blood, in land, in spirit.

SANA

Contents

"When I trust my voice to go where it needs to be, to find home, it returns to where it belongs, back to the source of its longing."

—Joy Harjo

Listening to Clouds

tell me the first name was the sound of beak against bamboo,
the sound of a tree splitting when we emerged nameless
sameness. One of us they called Crisostomo, and he became man.
One of us they called Maria Clara, and I became ghost.

I tell you I have two names. My parents wanted to double their chances,
give me two fates. They dreamt of me before I existed. Me, a vision
in piña, sitting on a high-back peacock throne, hair curling softly, demurely
weeping as I worked my fan, wind and water, goddess of small typhoons.

Taghirap closes like a crocodile's jaw clacking a tiny snap
of neck. I tell you the way to deal with separation is to pretend
there is nothing tragic about the fact that I can't speak
my grandparents' language, have no words for the day dims

distant in the playback of my mind. Every memory starts with you
had to be there, when I have no way to say this the way that I feel it.
I hold the feeling, the small clump of knowledge, an inch of earth
on a turtle's back, the gnawing awareness of perhaps

this is the piece hardest to let go. That nothing is how I remember.
Sarap is a manufactured beehive hum, gold plated palabok red-ringed
in violence. If every new story is a groundbreaking freedom,
it's time I walk the broken ground.

Crack the can of spam open: this is how you make war
rhyme with comfort. We eat the rations you didn't want and we drive
the cars you left to rust. Five hundred years ago you manifested,
a storm gathering at the end of the world. Trauma rolls fresh thunder

and the rain is salt on my tongue. No man is an island
because the island is a woman. I have been an island ever since
I first saw the ocean. Ever since a great bird flew me across the sea
dropped me into the snow and told me, this is what it means to be

alone. And I looked out across the winter white city
and the cold cut my black hair and tried to make me forget
the large mountain and the flowing river, the land of my name.
But I will keep searching for it. I tell myself I will find it.

This is the only way to reach you, when the sky is an uncrossable bridge
over an impossible ocean. Hinahanap is the breath escaping, a drip of red
slipping slowly from my nose. What an idea: in place of language, a rupture
of capillaries. The word still finds its way out.

I tell myself stories in order to live.
I emerge myself from jungle leaves.
I am a yellow head with horns.
I open my one thousand eyes.

I

"…through our people we learn how they have suffered; we learn from the first that came. And as a poet I sing their songs to the wind, to a thousand bursting suns, until we can all sit down and enjoy life with a bowl of rice and fish."

—Al Robles

How People Were Created

The first time, they tell you who you are.
They want you to be cornmeal
and scales, half-wild eyes,
ears and nose on a meaningless face.
Your limbs are useless, your hands
don't grasp anything at all.

Now, we try again. We give the body
shape. We move like fire
against wind. We have ears: listen
we have eyes: watch
our hands hold, our arms link—this
is the first history.

But we keep the scales on the tips of our fingers,
every touch a reminder,
a small threat.

Aubade

Each day, it is woman's work
to make the world.
Memory and dream mingle and fade
into the brightening sky. She,
with her walis tingting, sweeping
sleep from the concrete and clay
of the doorstep, bent down to coax kisses
upon the earth, wish-wishing
good morning, good morning.
Later in the afternoon, she will collect
chismis that the chirping birds have left
like offerings at the altar
of her window screen,
lace gardens of sampaguita together
for selling outside the church;
with any left over she might go to the station
or some other place that needs
a patron saint of hope and of goodbyes.
But for now, it is still early,
and she makes all the time in the world.
She bids me to come sit
at the kitchen table, where she tells me
the stories no one else hears
and the way to sing love
songs in another language. She laughs
and the sound is like jasmine
rice raining free and plenty
into the basket. We begin
the humble task of keeping time—
winnowing the clouds,
sifting through the grains of each day.

For Lola, Nanay, Ma, and all my Titas

What Did She Hear?

Was it the rising wind and worry that her sisters
wouldn't come back for her?
Was it his voice when he introduced himself, confident
he knew something she didn't?
Was it the murmur of life she carried, birthed, raised from silence
that calls to her now from the yard?
Was it the way her daughter's laugh was a river, the way
    it rushed quickly and carved deep lines into the earth of her heart,
        how it seemed never to start or to end
            as if it promised to carry her away if she let herself be
                lost to it?
How many wailing days, how many whispering nights were swallowed
in the folds of his old hunting bag? What was the sound
of her long-broken wings?

Brighter

It's always the golden boy who declares war
on his sister. Who was there to witness
the silver and steel in her skin
how she could fight

      and she could fight   and   fight   and   fight
I am no less
than you

      and how he could take what is not his and leave
      a hollowness
           an injury, a punishment.

          Justice is blind   so it goes
She would never see
an equal kingdom
there is no equal   king   dom
                  She would live on the dark side of the
story   nobody
      complains when the sun shines each morning   everybody is busy
      filling in their own craters

      nobody
      looks hard at the sun.

I smooth half my face in obligation   in the oblique night
      of forgetting
          the truth: when I sleep   I remember

in the long shadow of   memory is   *my right*   eye
                  I am owed.

Now Before Names

After Gwendolyn Brooks, after Terrance Hayes, after Joy Harjo

we real cool. we swing our arms to show off each rubber band,
                colors jangle on our wrists. we

know what we want we can get for a clap and a song,
                tatay gusto ko'ng tinapay, we sing

or we chase the taho man. the sun pulls oceans out our skin,
                bodies of water and asin

make nanay pinch her lips, pa kiss-kiss naman.
                she stuffs towels down our shirts and we

dance away, we full-fledged gravity defiers,
                masked heroes and bandits flying to the thin

green edge that jungles up at the end of the kalye,
                past always-parked cars marking the origin

of species, where all creatures of the earth are
                frogs & ants & spiders & dragonflies & we

are bony elbows and muddy knees, limbs stretching, spiking
                up trees, brown feet beating jazz

and not jazz, i wasn't american yet. now is a promise
                of longsilog lunch, the endless ilog of june

afternoons. now is not time. now is a trumpet
                sprawl, is tarat tarat tarat, is tara tara na, is we.

War is a Woman's Body

War is a woman's body.
We watch the house wrap itself around her.
Light and heat return to the earth.
An ember glows itself into a tree.
We pick the fruit to eat it.
This we call Peace.

Prayer to My Ancestors

The name of the father, and of the son, and of the holy spirit
are not your names—I pray in the language of the people

who killed the people who killed the people who killed
you—you who were strong with old magic, who wielded our stories,

the buntot pagi for whipping wayward aswang—the sinturon
is a reminder—the pain that unwinds from your waist is the sting

of our story—you intend to carve topography into your landless child,
pink pooling across my skin to form islands, red running in rivers

you draw me a map to my inheritance—the world promised, the world lost,
the world left—at least, this was what you hoped

and if there was another way, you didn't see it—bad eyesight, like pain,
is a thing we share. our only bridge in a widening sea

where I am no pagi—I forget more every day, and that is a quiet grave
robbery—if I said, mano po—would you bless me

what is a body in pain but a prayer—what are our hands but our trauma:
palms open, asking and asking

Portrait of the Artist as Manananggal

I.

Portrait of the artist as manananggal. Of manananggal as ghazal. How do I name this skin? When in the end I am not art and everything is a monster?

Jackfruit cracked yellow jewels of skin. Rotting meat belly stretched ready
for blood. Bully among classmates. Blessed art Thou amongst monsters.[1]

I am a winged child spilled in half, drowning my blood in the work, twisting tongue around pregnant pauses. My hands open the last can of Monster.

Tonight, the dim ways of kiss: the chiming hands, the ribcage gates of Troy. Savage
her body to the pale clocks. My tongue's a long scar they mistake for monster.[2]

I fly over the rooftops of all the places I came from. My wings rupture the pale moon, casting new shapes over the sleeping heads of conquered monsters.

Astride sea gates, the imprisoned Mother of Exiles conquering
limb and name. Give me your tired, your tempest, your teeming monsters.[3]

Buwan, a river rock skips across the sea: moon,

the concentric haloes of our stories

II

"We tell ourselves stories in order to live."

—Joan Didion

II.

Portrait of ghazal as found poem. Portrait of found poem as severed name.
Portrait of name as given history. History as blackout. Blackout as monster.

History is a hideous female severing intestines, sprouting huge. The Tagalog separates
itself. Crushed by sunrise. The west, salt and holy. Takot ka ba sa monster?[4]

Saltwater gulps at my toes, smooths the hard edge of remembering. Fate
is crossing water when we die. The land forgets: we are each other's monsters.

Where is the dark rich land we wanted to wander? Subway train lurching, hatred
passed through. Machinery of memory, a harshness. My monster.[5]

Tear me through the middle like paper. Throw my heart to the jungle, my feet
to desert. This way I am loved and lost, living like mother's exiled monster.

So much an address it was like something living. Years after, you do not know
what the address was. It is not a name, not a thing that exists, but some monster.[6]

House of Santelmo

A daughter is a burning candle.
My mother shakes her head,
a white hair for every day I was
a bad child and made her angry.
My job was to pluck them out,
undo the damage done.

A white hair is a wick of dynamite.
I light the ends of my white hairs,
singe them to black. Flames crawl
up the nape of my neck, sizzle
in my ears, and wash my skull in light.

An ate is an apparition in the fog.
I move in migration patterns
swamped in disappointment
hoping this place won't kill me.
I walk across the threshold, scorch
black footprints into carpet.

A day is a box of collected regrets.
I bring my mistakes with me
bubble-wrapped and stacked
like fractures up a spine. I carry them
up a flight of stairs, back burning.

An apartment is a history of empire,
each room a world domination.
My bookshelves go up in flame.
The eggshell paint becomes
charcoal and petroleum,
forests of paper thin dinosaurs
hatching, dying, fossilizing.

A housewarming is a warding
of evil. But holy water, like good
intention, is a thing that seeps
and rusts and ruins. We bless
this house, knowing our demons
gather in the dark corners, ready
to follow us to the next place.

If a family is utang na loob
then is a home the tableau
of how we fail one another?

A Pinay is an angry spirit
constantly burning, always
in some state of packing
and leaving. A body threatened
and threatening to disappear
into the whitening horizon,
the way lightning leaves
a scar of memory on the sea.

Ballad of the Trickster

The government had removed all the bodies from the desert, except for the skulls of the giants worn smooth by rain and time. The first ghosts arrived on a pirate ship. It came out of the fog and when the fog left, it didn't. Then men started singing cowboy songs and mass-producing ghost towns. You wouldn't see the ghost towns unless you went looking.

At night the dogs prowl for campfires, sniffing for us. They are afraid when we gather, afraid when we shake hands. The hills conspire with us. We carve codes into the rock faces, trade in songs on the black market, whistle and hum in pitches they can't hear. How to give ourselves love. They are afraid of what we know.

Every so often, we see our faces on the news. We are wanted for being unwanted. They chase us, we shapeshift and escape each time. We're spiders, we're foxes with many tails. We're tikbalang, the way we run so far and fast we confound them. We jackrabbit down the dirt roads, laughing at them.

They call us stranger, outlaw, enemy. They don't know our real names. They can't understand me when I say to them: I am a mountain; I am a wind so wild it flows like freedom; I was born in a volcano; I come from a hundred lands. When I say these words, only the ones who have lost something, too, can understand. We nod to one another, they don't see. They think it is only a myth. And the black market grows.

Let the dogs howl. Tonight the sky covers us, that old crow's wing. Tonight the stars twinkle their secrets at us. Remember us, we are coming back to you. And we have shifted again. Tonight we are sampaguita pushing up from the skulls of sleeping giants, growing a new planet, shining as bright as the stars.

The Girl Who Became a Cactus

i've been in southern california so long
i've become a cactus
the santa ana winds howl around me
desert grit roots me in place

there's a layer of dust on my crocodile skin
i've been in southern california so long
the hawk cuts an arc in the sky and agrees
i've become a cactus

the santa ana winds howl around me
chasing the cars' wild roar through the basin
desert grit roots me in place
of the water i came from—split my scales

to see the soft coconut flesh surviving
like a river under years and years of sun

In the Last Days of the Kingdom

The plane idles on the tarmac, heavy and bloated as a beached whale
    The subway is a hollow snakeskin
The unfinished freeway undoes itself, decaying
    wood beams exposed like bones jutting from carcass.

On the street the people walk quickly, dark heads bowed, faces covered.
    They say nothing to one another, make no eye contact, knowing
      each stare can become steel, a knife to the face.

A nurse collapses in the break room.
    Death makes rounds through the hallways, knocking softly on doors
      of the old ones waiting for a visit.

The rich gather inside a mansion of marble and alabaster
    They sip on crystal champagne glasses full of bleach
      to become white on the inside, too.

They bury the nurse.

Semi-trucks are parked
    on the side of the road. Inside their trailers, bodies
      heaped and rotting: the cemeteries are full.

The car groans into the driveway like an old dog searching for someplace to die.

And she talks to herself in an empty room
and his hair grows long and his body curves to the shape of the table
and their noses sting from the alcohol
and their palms turn slick
and their knuckles raw
      from washing
        their clothes by hand
      from washing
        off the careless coughs of others
      from washing
        the day from every last cell of skin

Over the shuffle of papers, of sound
        mind and body, they listen
                for the phone to give news.

                                        The ones behind glass
                                        wish for home.

Each minute is a question: Am I ready to head this house?
                            Am I ready to support all the families back home?
                            Am I ready to die?

A skyline cuts uneven teeth
                an animal's mouth in one long and pleading gasp

Meryenda

Ma slices the mango into three parts. I'll show you a trick.
She cups one portion and scores straight lines into the fruit,
horizontal then vertical. Her fingers push softly upward
into the mango skin, invert the bowl shape and the fruit
erupts like a firework, spikes out in all directions.
My sister and I applaud this magic show. A crown, Ma says.
She gives it to my sister and makes the second for me,
a halo this time. My nose fills with sweetness,
lips purse around one ray of sun. I kiss and disappear
yellow flesh. It tastes different in New Jersey. Ma keeps
the center, smallest, thinnest. It is her favorite part
—the way the fish head is her favorite part
(she sucks out one eyeball, then the other)
the way the burnt edge is her favorite part
(she scrapes the brown off our rice)—
Ma peels her core, the golden
ring around the hard patch
pale as an exposed chest.
She bites, cleaves heart
from bone. She smiles
like she enjoys
herself.

If You Want to Know Where I'm Really From, I'll Tell You

I come from a universe where the men have beer and gasoline in their veins
and swagger around as if always on the verge of spontaneously combusting.
The backs of their hands are the deep cracked leather of a steering wheel
tanned by the long afternoon. When the sun sinks down behind the anarchy
of buildings, a thousand new suns floodlight up, selling Bench or Jollibee or
the latest movie. I marvel at how they navigate this galaxy, the spiral-armed
barangay networks. Each jeepney is a rocket to the moon, fins and flags
streaming, chrome-skinned and tattooed with dragons & eagles & tigers &
the Virgin Mary. The sari-sari storefronts are still open at this hour,
part business part backyard, where the elderly sit watching dramas unfold
on small TVs resting on the counter, and the young ones holler around on
their quicker knees. The scents of rotisserie chicken and fried fishballs
reach my passenger window. Our rosary hangs on the rearview mirror,
beads catching the twinkle off streetlamps. At every bump in the road
Jesus is a spaceman doing ollies in the air for us; and I brace myself
against the handle like I'll go to hell for that joke, but I inherited my kulit
from these men who scatter like ashes like stars across darkness,
zigzagging their shine through Manila traffic out to California, to New
York, to Saudi; out where young men go and become old men. I count down
turns in roads with the names of soldiers & saints & American states &
I'm gazing out at myself, visible only once every few years, wingtip
blink of memory or ball of fire shedding my selves again, again. Here
our van growls upon re-entry into the driveway. The dog is leashed up
beyond the iron gate and the laundry on the line waves us in, a collection
of flags in celebration. We spill out like a sigh where we touch down to earth,
bellies full of food, thoughts already on the mattress on the cool tile floor,
the swaying fan's lullaby hum. On the wall, a butiki defies gravity, eyes me
a moment, then ultimately moves on, one traveler understanding another.

For Lolo, Tatay, Dad, and all my Titos

Tomorrow is a Long Way Back

Follow your dog into the forest. Walk
where the trees grow gnarled and wild, misted
thickly with ancient coolness. No one remembers
the last breath that warmed this place. The dog knows
the way.

The tree trunks knot themselves around you
as you venture in, lattices for the weaving vine and creeping
moss. Sunlight dapples softly, then sparsely, then
snuffs out altogether. You begin to lose your sense
of time, in this quiet room in the heart
of the earth. This is incidental, and this is fine.
You shed your time like old skin
with every exhale. Create yourself
with every inhale. Mark your passage
with footprints dropped like grains of sand in the glass.
Keep walking,
you will find it.

The city shines as if made of sky. Its lights, so many mirrors
waiting.

That we are here
is a myth.

III

Notes & Acknowledgements

Publisher's Note

The Tagalog phrases found throughout the collection are translated into English in the following Translation Index.

We translate these phrases into English for inclusivity purposes in respect to our non-Tagalog speaking readers, particularly BIPOC and non-Tagalog Filipinxao readers. We also translate these phrases in order to adhere to the requirements set by some book distributors.

We are aware of the compromise we make in order to make this art more accessible to a wider audience. In translating these phrases, we participate in a global market that continues to be dictated by Western- and English-supremacist practices. We are also aware that these simple, direct translations of words fall short in communicating their cultural weight and meaning.

We acknowledge the history of translating devices used violently as tools of white gaze revisionism, for the cultural erasure and othering of non-Western, Global South, and diaspora art. This includes the related practice in the United States publishing industry of italicizing words from non-English languages. Our current policy is not to italicize these words.

As cultural discourse, translation methods, and language resources evolve with the times, so may our formatting and translating practices at Sampaguita Press. It is our dream and goal to be able to have our titles commercially available and translated into different languages other than English, for greater language and literary equity.

Translation Index

The page numbers follow the print edition of *Sana*.

Sana (title page): An expression of hope and wishing; "if only"

Sampaguita (title page): A Jasmine flower native to South and Southeast Asia; the national flower of the Philippines

Kaibigan (5): Friend

Piña (14): A traditional fiber made from the leaves of the pineapple plant used for weaving lustrous lace-like luxury textiles

Taghirap (14): Hardship

Sarap (14): Delicious, deliciousness

Palabok (14): A rice noodle dish

Hinahanap (15): Searching

Lola (20): Grandmother

Nanay (20): Mother; in this case, the name I call my maternal lola

Tita (20): Aunt

Walis tingting (20): A household broom for outdoor use

Chismis (20): Gossip

Tatay gusto ko'ng tinapay (24): A phrase from a children's hand clapping game; "Father, I want bread"

Taho (24): Snack food made of silken tofu, tapioca pearls, and syrup

Asin (24): Salt

Nanay (24): Mother

Pa kiss-kiss naman (24): Roughly translated, "Give me a kiss"

Kalye (24): Street

Longsilog (24): A dish usually served for breakfast or lunch, consisting of longganisa sausage, garlic rice, and eggs

Ilog (24): River

Tarat tarat tarat (24): A trumpet-like sound effect evoking playfulness, used in popular songs

Tara tara na (24): "Let's go, let's go"

Buntot pagi (26): A stingray tail used as a weapon to protect against aswang

Pagi (26): Stingray

Aswang (26): Monster, demon

Sinturon (26): Belt

Mano po (26): Asking an elder for their hand in order to receive a blessing

Manananggal (28): A winged monster in the form of a woman that can detach at the torso; it feeds on sleeping people, particularly unborn babies and pregnant women

Buwan (29): Moon

Takot ka ba sa monster? (32): "Are you afraid of monsters?"

Santelmo (33): Derived from "St. Elmo's Fire"; a monster or spirit made of fire that appears to sailors on the ocean and travelers in bogs and swamps

Ate (33): Older sister

Utang na loob (34): Literally translated, "Debt from inside" / "Debt of inner (self)"; a complicated cultural value of deep social obligation, most commonly applied to family and close friends

Pinay (34): A colloquialism derived from "Pilipina"

Tikbalang (36): A "werehorse" with a human body, long limbs, and the head and hooves of a horse; in stories, the hero's goal is often to capture the tikbalang and force it into servitude

Meryenda (40): A snack often had in the afternoon, before dinner

Lolo (41): Grandfather

Tatay (41): Father; in this case, the name I call my maternal lolo

Tito (41): Uncle

Barangay (41): The smallest administrative division in the Philippines, roughly equated to a village or district; in large metropolitan areas, the term is often applied to neighborhoods and suburbs

Jeepney (41): The most popular form of public transportation in the Philippines, similar in function to a bus; derived in part from the repurposing of military jeeps left behind by the US around World War II

Sari-sari store (41): A small neighborhood convenience store that is most commonly family-run out of the shopkeeper's residence

Kulit (41): Stubbornness, mischief, an air of disobedience often with a childlike energy

Butiki (41): Small geckos or lizards commonly found in houses, usually seen climbing up walls

Author's Notes

I.   Alternate versions of the following poems were published, or have been accepted for forthcoming publication, in the following literary magazines. My heartfelt thanks to all of these publications for welcoming my work.

Listening to Clouds — *All My Relations*
How People Were Created — *Chopsticks Alley Pinoy*, *Marías at Sampaguitas*
Aubade, Ballad of the Trickster — *Fahmidan Journal*
Brighter — *CP Quarterly*
Now Before Names — *Touchstone Literary Magazine*
Portrait of the Artist as Manananggal (parts I & II) — *Sage Cigarettes*
House of Santelmo — *Yuzu Press*
In the Last Days of the Kingdom — *the winnow*
Meryenda — *Cut Fruit Stories Vol. 1*, *Marías at Sampaguitas*
If you want to know where I'm really from, I'll tell you — *decomp journal*
Tomorrow is a Long Way Back — *Antigone*
War is a Woman's Body, What Did She Hear?, The Girl Who Became a Cactus — *Marías at Sampaguitas*

II.   The following poems were inspired by stories from *Philippine Myths, Legends, and Folktales* by Maximo D. Ramos:

How People Were Created — "How People Were Created"
What Did She Hear? — "The Tale of Magbaloto"
Brighter — "Why the Sun is Brighter than the Moon"
War is a Woman's Body — "The Origin of Bananas"
Tomorrow is a Long Way Back — "The Man Who Reached the Sky-World"

III.   "Now Before Names" is a golden shovel poem that uses long lines. Due to the constraints of the printed page dimensions, these lines have been cut in half. For free access to the original long-line poem, please see its publication in *Touchstone Literary Magazine* Spring 2021 issue. The golden shovel is a form invented by Terrance Hayes with his poem, "The Golden Shovel," and used by Joy Harjo in "An American Sunrise." Both poets pay homage to Gwendolyn Brooks's "We Real Cool," and I have continued in that tradition.

IV. The italicized couplets in "Portrait of the Artist as Manananggal" Parts I and II are found poetry. Each couplet was composed using a different work:

1. "Blessed Fruit" by Isabel Garcia-Gonzales, *Kuwento: Lost Things*
2. "Lorca's Red Dresses" by Natalie Diaz, *When My Brother was an Aztec*
3. "The New Colossus" by Emma Lazarus
4. Wikipedia entry: "Manananggal"
5. "Eye to Eye: Black Women, Hatred, and Anger" by Audre Lorde, *Sister Outsider*
6. Excerpt of a letter by Gertrude Stein, *Everybody's Autobiography*

V. "Ballad of the Trickster" was written in response to and support of the #NoBackgroundChecksNeeded open mic series organized in October 2021 by Santa Clara County Poet Laureate Janice Lobo Sapigao and Honorary Poet Laureates Keana Aguila Labra and Lorenz Dumuk. The series gathered poets in solidarity to protest the use of background checks in the application process for SCC Poet Laureate. This practice disproportionately targets and excludes people from specific communities that have histories of deep harm under police systems, such as Black writers, Indigenous writers, writers of color, and undocumented writers.

VI. "The Girl Who Became a Cactus" is a labra poem, a form invented by poet Keana Aguila Labra.

VII. The quotes found at the beginning of the chapbook sections are from the following works:

1. Joy Harjo's quote is from her essay, "Every Poem Has Ancestors," published in *The Paris Review*. The essay is an excerpt from her memoir, *Poet Warrior*.
2. Al Robles' quote is from his essay, "Hanging on to the Carabao's Tail," originally published in *Amerasia Journal* and re-published in his collection, *Rappin' with Ten Thousand Carabaos in the Dark*.
3. Joan Didion's quote is from the title essay of her collection, *The White Album*.

Acknowledgements

All my thanks to the following:

To Luya Poetry, Walang Hiya Project, Poet Laureate Santa Clara County, *Nomadic Press*, *Fahmidan Journal*, and *the winnow* who have provided spaces for my work to be performed, always to the warmest welcome.

To the instructors of the workshops I took throughout 2020 and 2021, who provided community in this era of social distance: Jason Bayani of Kearny Street Workshop, Barbara Jane Reyes, and Karo Ska with Asian American Justice + Innovation Lab.

To some of my first literary teachers from years ago, the student instructors, lecturers, visiting artists, and professors at UC Berkeley; I hope I can advocate for young artists the way you all did for me: Nadia Ellis, Robert Hass, Lyn Hejinian, Lili Loofbourow, John Shoptaw, Catherine Walsh.

To artists Francesca Alarcon, Miriam Mosqueda, Risa Wright, and Zlivkun, whose art captured the essence of this chapbook even before they read any of the poems, which maybe speaks to how we artists can dream in parallel. To my pinsan Einreb Kal Regoso, for the spirit and talent you brought to this project, and for showing me how fun it is to make art with family.

To the following friends, who generously devoted your time and effort as Beta Readers and Blurb Writers; thank you for holding my work and letting me in: Francesca Alarcon, Hari Alluri, Zachary FR Anderson, Isabel Angeles, Tesia Blanton, Chris L. Butler, Nicole Cadelina, Nikki Liv Casta Basas, Rachael Crosbie, Nathalie De Los Santos, Melissa Gill, Diana Hîncu, Pilar Huerta, Roxanne Lim, Janice Lobo Sapigao, Ellie Lopez, Angelo Lorenzo, Jason Magabo Perez, Jennifer Nessel, Khalisa Rae, Tiffany Tarampi, Czaerra Galicinao Ucol, AV.

To the friends and readers who will review the ARC, or who will buy a copy and review this book in the future: thank you so much for your support, and for giving me faith that we're succeeding in making more and more room for the voices of brown artists.

To the groups and artists who will collaborate with me to amplify *Sana*, who I've yet to meet: I'm no less grateful to you. I can't wait to meet you and see what we do together.

To Nashira de la Rosa, Asela Lee Kemper, Dina Klarisse, Noreen Ocampo, and Kelly Ritter: I couldn't have asked for better kumares to lead this radical publishing group. To mare Keana Aguila Labra, for being in my corner for this book and this Press, from day one. When I grow up, I wanna be a Virgo.

To my Anderson and Bolaños families here in the US; to my extended family living and working overseas, so many so scattered that I don't even really know where you are; to the Montemayor & Bolaños families in the Philippines; to the elders we lost to Covid-19; to the babies born and growing up in this time; all love.

Sa mga pinsan ko: RJ, Jon, Mark, Justin, Jhel, Rommel, Rennan, Enah, Ericka, Mauro, Miguel, Jemarick, Jmarc, Kurt, Brian, Annie, Amie, Geno, Gabriel, Dhaniel. I miss you, as always. To your fiances, spouses, and children who make this list joyously longer: I can't wait to see you and meet you.

Sa mga tita & tito ko: Beth & Charles, Roy & Meli, Liza & Rene, Rey & Bebe, Ricky & Myra, Malyn, Tina, Arman & Fhannie. Thank you for the tsismis, facetime, and fb messages that keep us close. Thank you for hosting all the homecomings at the heart of my memories.

Kay Lola & Lolo, at Nanay & Tatay: Maraming salamat po para sa ating pamilya. Thank you for making this family. At maraming salamat po para sa mga kwento ninyo. I keep them alive.

To Michele and Raymond who lived many of these poems with me. May there be more poems in store for us.

To Ma and Dad, who told me all of my first stories, who gave me all of my first books, who are the source of my language. I don't thank you enough.

To David. ILYB.

About the Author

Maria Bolaños (she/her/they) is a Filipina American poet, co-Editor in Chief for *Marías at Sampaguitas* magazine, and co-Founder & -Publisher of Sampaguita Press. She is committed to building spaces to nurture and showcase Filipinxao literature as well as Black, Indigenous, and POC literature.

Maria studied English Literature, Media Studies, and Creative Writing at UC Berkeley. She was nominated for the 2021-2022 Best of the Net Anthology, and their poems are featured in US-based publications and organizations such as *Touchstone Literary Magazine*, Cut Fruit Collective's *Cut Fruit Stories*, and *decomp journal*, among others; as well as international publications such as South Africa-based *Antigone* and Singapore-based *Yuzu Press*. Maria also writes reviews for the Seattle-based pan-Asian Pacific American publication, *International Examiner*, and runs a bookstagram account, @mariabeewrites.

Born in Manila, with family roots from the provinces of Pangasinan, Bulacan, Sorsogon, and Quezon, Maria immigrated to the United States in childhood and has lived on both the East and West Coasts. She currently lives with her husband in Tovaangar, the unceded Gabrielino, Tongva, and Kizh land also known as Los Angeles, California.

About the Artists

The page numbers follow the print edition of *Sana*.

Book Cover Art: "Sayang at Sana" by Francesca Alarcon

21: Zlivkun is an Indonesia-based artist who specializes in surreal, sci-fi, or fantasy style. Zlivkun's work is inspired by Japanese culture, the Victorian age, ancient tribes and myths across the world. See their portfolio and gigs at fiverr.com/zlivkun.

27: Risa Wright (she/her) is a graphic designer and illustration artist. You can follow Risa's designs and illustrations on Instagram, @risa.wright.

35: Einreb Kal "Reb" Regoso is a 20-year-old Fine Arts Student at University of the Philippines Diliman. Most of his works are inspired by Surrealist artists H.R. Giger and Zdzisław Beksiński. His preferred media are oil paint, colored pencil, crafting (prop making and masks), and digital arts. He's fond of using dark tones to emphasize the details and depth of his works to make the viewer experience his inner feelings while creating his craft. Reb is currently creating masterpieces to fulfill his goal of having a one-man exhibit. For now some of his works can be seen on YouTube and Instagram, @ev_regoso.

43: Art by Miriam Mosqueda, Instagram @vientoxsol

Land Acknowledgement

This book was written on the lands of the Gabrielino, Tongva, and Kizh People, and the Chumash People. It was produced on the lands of the Ohlone People.

As settlers on Turtle Island, the staff at Sampaguita Press acknowledge we are on the stolen sacred lands of these Peoples. We remember their connection to these regions and give thanks for the opportunity to live, teach, and learn in their traditional homelands. May we create connections with them, and may we learn Indigenous protocols to become honorable stewards of the land.

We encourage you, Reader, to:

- Amplify the voices of Indigenous people leading grassroots change movements
- Donate your time and money to Indigenous-led organizations
- Politically support the Land Back Movement

In line with these encouragements, Sampaguita Press supports Indigenous art and donates a portion of Press funds raised to Indigenous-led organizations.

In reflecting on our own lives and remembering our family histories, we must remember the legacies of colonialism that we have benefitted from and continue to benefit from as settler-colonialists.

From Palestine to the Philippines, none of us are free until all of us are free.

About Sampaguita Press

Sampaguita Press is an independent micropress publishing house based in San Jose, California. We publish works by and for Black, Indigenous, and POC artists. We acknowledge the intersections of identity and support the LGBTQIA+ folk/x in the Black, Indigenous, and POC communities as well.

Sampaguita Press was founded in 2021 by poets and creatives who wanted to create a space and platform for ourselves, our peers, and other fellow voices who are underrepresented in mainstream publishing.

We strive to inspire progressive change. We acknowledge that change is made with solidarity. We honor and nurture the relationships between our fellow communities. We especially seek works that broaden perspectives and foster understanding.

We believe in racial and social equity. We acknowledge that Western literature and publishing are still overwhelmingly white spaces, and we are committed to amplifying underrepresented voices by providing attention and care to artists who may not have access to traditional publishing spaces.

We are an intersectionally feminist & womanist, inclusive press. We prioritize Black, Indigenous, and POC artists of all genders. We discourage hegemonic narratives; hierarchical structures; and supremacist, assimilationist, and normative messaging.

We are a safe literary & linguistic space, and we welcome chapbook submissions in non-English languages.

We support Indigenous rights and sovereignty over the land known as the United States. Our support goes out to the Indigenous groups everywhere in the world who have been harmed, silenced, and displaced. We encourage our readers to learn about and support Indigenous Peoples.

Look for the next title from
Sampaguita Press

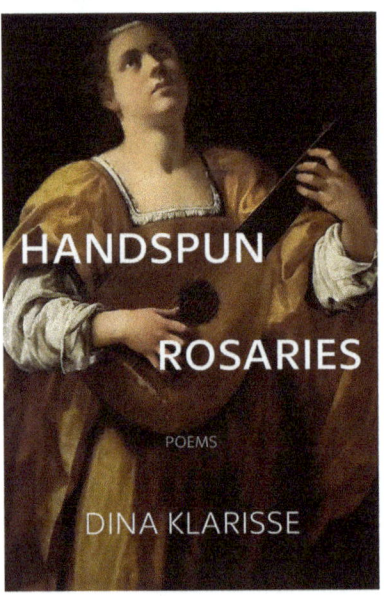

HANDSPUN ROSARIES by Dina Klarisse

Handspun Rosaries is the communion of a lapsed Catholic, the memories and reflections of a Filipina American immigrant raised to internalize the colonial heritage of her Christian-centric society. In these poems, Dina Klarisse weaves prayer and narrative into a lifelong interrogation of God: she scavenges for the remnants of faith in identity, reminisces on family rituals, questions the dogmatic monsterization of women—and ultimately invites us to look for a new, expanded horizon of belief and faith.

Visit www.SampaguitaPress.com to learn more.

www.ingramcontent.com/pod-product-compliance
Lightning Source LLC
Chambersburg PA
CBHW051648120626
46551CB00015B/2260